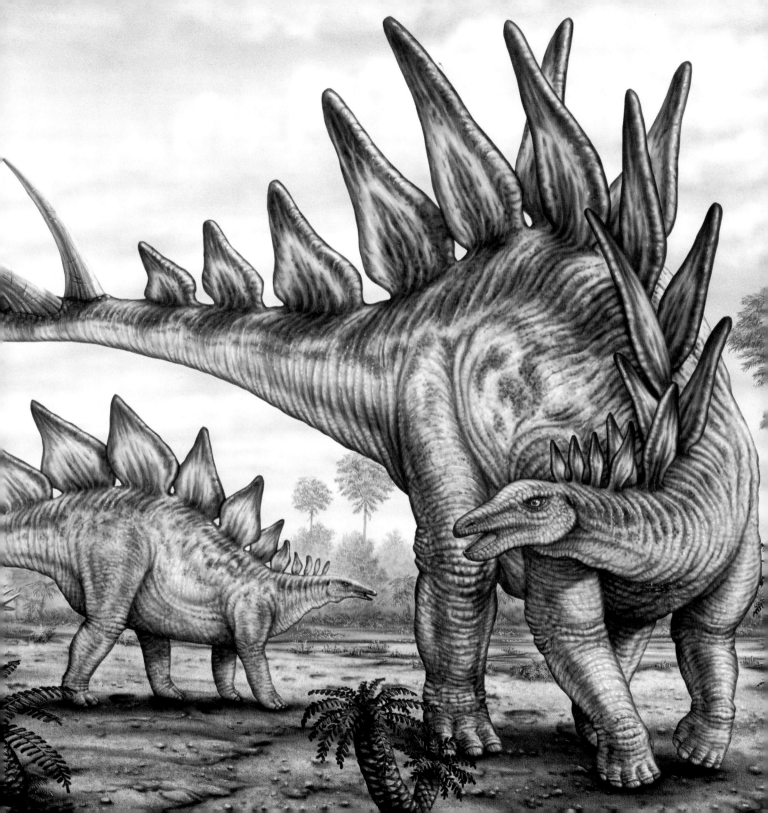

Published by Smart Apple Media
1980 Lookout Drive, North Mankato, Minnesota 56003
Produced by Byron Preiss Visual Publications, Inc.

Cover design by Dean Motter
Interior design by Gilda Hannah
Edited by Howard Zimmerman

Front and back cover art by Phil Wilson

Art Credits: Pages 1, 5, 7 © 2002 Phil Wilson. Page 3 © 2002 Berislav Krzic. Pages 8, 25 © 2002 John Sibbick. Page 13 © 2002 Douglas Henderson. Pages 9, 16 © 2002 Gregory S. Paul. Page 11 © 2002 Rich Penney. Pages 14–15, 18, 20 © 2002 Patrick O'Brien. Page 19 © 2002 Christopher Srnka. Pages 21, 26, 27 © 2002 Jan Sovak. Pages 22–23 © 2002 Mark Hallett. Page 28 © 2002 Michael Carroll. Pages 29, 31 © 2002 Alex Ebel.

Printed in the U.S.A.

Library of Congress Cataloging-in-Publication Data

Olshevsky, George.
Stegosaurus / by George Olshevsky and Sandy Fritz.
p. cm.—(Discovering dinosaurs)
Summary: Presents information on *Stegosaurus*, including physical
characteristics, diet, habitat, known social organization, close relatives,
and areas where fossils have been found.
ISBN 1-58340-179-2
1. Stegosaurus—Juvenile literature. [1. Stegosaurus. 2. Dinosaurs.]
I. Fritz, Sandy. II. Title.
QE862.O65 O48 2002
567.915'3—dc21   2002017633

First Edition

2 4 6 8 9 7 5 3 1

3/03   12607

STEGOSAURUS

Sandy Fritz and George Olshevsky

SMART APPLE MEDIA

Dinosaurs lived on Earth from about 227 million to 65 million years ago. Scientists call this the Mesozoic era. It is also called the Age of Reptiles or the Age of Dinosaurs. Dinosaurs were closely related to today's reptiles and birds. In fact, many scientists now think that birds evolved from a small meat-eating dinosaur that was a swift runner. All dinosaurs were land animals. Flying reptiles (called pterosaurs) and reptiles that swam in the sea also lived during this period, but they were not dinosaurs.

The Age of Dinosaurs, the Mesozoic era, is divided into three periods. The earliest period is called the Triassic, which lasted from 248 million to 205 million years ago. Dinosaurs first appeared around the middle of this period. The Jurassic period followed, lasting from 205 million to 145 million years ago. The final period is called the Cretaceous. The Cretaceous spanned from 145 million to 65 million years ago. After the Cretaceous, dinosaurs were gone.

But during their time, dinosaurs lived everywhere on Earth, even in Antarctica. About 700 different kinds of dinosaurs have been unearthed, and many more remain in the ground awaiting discovery. There were meat-eating dinosaurs that could run fast on their long hind legs. There were four-legged, plant-eating dinosaurs 150 feet (46 m) long and weighing as much as 100 tons (91 t)! There were dinosaurs with horns, crests, and bony armor. Some dinosaurs, both meat-eaters and plant-eaters, were as small as chickens or house cats.

Everything we know about dinosaurs comes from fossils that people have dug up from the ground. Scientists examine, measure, and analyze these fossils. From them we can learn when and where dinosaurs lived. We have learned how dinosaurs walked and ran, what they hunted, and what plants they ate. We can even figure out how long they lived. Presented in this series is the most up-to-date information we have learned about dinosaurs. We hope you'll enjoy reading all about the fabulous beasts of Earth's distant past.

Meet Stegosaurus

Stegosaurus walked much like an elephant. It was longer than two rhinos and weighed a bit more than one. And of course there were the bony plates. Nearly all members of the stegosaurid family had bony plates along their backs, and all had spikes at the ends of their tails. But no stegosaurid was bigger, or had bigger plates, than *Stegosaurus*.

Stegosaurus and most of its relatives lived about 145 million years ago, during the late Jurassic. *Stegosaurus* shared the landscape with several famous dinosaurs. Giant, plant-eating sauropods such as *Apatosaurus* and *Diplodocus* walked with *Stegosaurus*. Meat-eaters such as *Allosaurus* and *Ceratosaurus* also roamed the late Jurassic world.

During the late Jurassic, the stegosaurid family became quite diverse, with different arrangements of plates and spikes. These fossil finds could mean that

Could there have been a "second brain" that controlled the complex movements of *Stegosaurus*? In 1884, an enlargement was found along *Stegosaurus's* spinal column. The cavity seemed like it could have held the so-called second brain. Scientists now believe the cavity held a group of nerves that helped coordinate the animal's walking and tail-swinging.

Tall and narrow, plated and spiked, *Stegosaurus* was the largest member of its family of plant-eating dinosaurs.

This page: Members of the stegosaurid family show different arrangements of plates and spikes. Opposite page: *Stegosaurus* **is the only member of its family to have 17 plates along its back as well as spikes. Here is** *Huayangosaurus,* **one of the stegosaurids with long shoulder spikes.**

stegosaurids lived in a variety of environments. Each group may have acted differently and eaten different kinds of plants.

The basic design of stegosaurids was that of solid, probably slow-moving animals. Attach a small head to a medium-long neck. Attach the neck to a long, but fairly narrow, body with its tallest point being above the hips. Power the body's movement with massive hind legs. Add plates and spikes and armor. This is the recipe for making a stegosaurid.

Early stegosaurids had a modest development of plates and spikes. Some later stegosaurids, such as *Kentrosaurus*, were covered in formidable spikes. As a group, most stegosaurids grew to between 15 and 25 feet (4.5–7.6 m) long. They were long and low to the ground.

Most stegosaurids had spikes on their shoulders as well as on their backs and tails. *Stegosaurus* was the exception in the family. It had no shoulder spikes. It was also far taller at the hips than other stegosaurids, and it was covered with an extensive display of plates. Other stegosaurids had plates, too. But none were as large or as developed as the plates of *Stegosaurus*.

Stegosaurus stood 12 feet (3.6 m) high at the hips and could stretch up to 30 feet (9 m) long. It was narrow rather than squat. A 30-foot-long (9 m) dinosaur that weighs only two tons (1.8 t) is pretty light by dinosaur standards. And scientists don't think *Stegosaurus* was very bright. Its brain was the size of a walnut.

The animal supported its weight on thick, heavy legs that resembled those of a modern elephant. *Stegosaurus* probably walked like an elephant and may have managed a fast trot for short distances.

Stegosaurus's tail arched upward and was powerfully muscled. Two pairs of spikes stuck out from the end of the tail. *Stegosaurus* probably used its spikes to strike back at an attacking predator.

Like all dinosaurs, *Stegosaurus* may have been colored or patterned to blend into its environment. We have no evidence that it traveled in herds. Most fossil finds are of isolated individuals rather than groups.

This illustration of *Stegosaurus* shows off its 17 plates and high tail with four spikes.

Stegosaurus's World

To understand *Stegosaurus*, scientists look at the world it lived in 145 million years ago. The level of the seas was high. This flooded low-lying land and put a lot of moisture into the air. Hot, tropical climates dominated the northern half of the world. Rainfall was plentiful. This climate supported rich plant growth. It was this abundant plant life in the late Jurassic that fed giant herbivores such as stegosaurids and sauropods.

Many *Stegosaurus* fossils have been found in ancient river channels. The finds are usually mixed with the fossil bones of other animals. But the *Stegosaurus* fossils show signs of having decayed in an open, dry area before being buried. It's possible that these dinosaurs died some distance from the water. Later, their bones could have been swept to the river by powerful flash floods.

Those Mysterious Plates

One of *Stegosaurus*'s most remarkable features was the plates running along its neck and back. Seventeen plates ran almost the full length of this dinosaur's spine. But enough room was left for the two pairs of horn-like spikes sticking out sideways near the tip of the tail. Neither spikes nor plates were directly attached to the animal's skeleton. Rather, they were bony extensions anchored in the animal's tough hide.

A group of *Stegosaurus* stops at a river for a drink at the edge of a conifer forest.

A male *Stegosaurus* issues a warning cry to others to keep out of his territory.

Stegosaurus's tall spine bones anchored a network of muscles that supported the plates. The latest fossil evidence seems to show that the plates were in two alternating rows. One plate stuck out to the left, the next stuck out to the right, and so on.

It's unlikely that *Stegosaurus*'s plates were defensive armor. They were very thin. Under the surface, networks of blood vessels cover the plates. Some scientists think the plates helped the dinosaur to control its body temperature. Flat to the sun, the plates would have absorbed warmth. When hot, the creature may have turned its face into the breeze. This would have guided cooling air along a channel between the plates.

Stegosaurus's plates may not have been used for defense, but the animal still had a good system of defensive shields. A beautifully preserved *Stegosaurus* found in Colorado in 1992 provided evidence of this. It retained almost all of the armor plating where it had been in life.

Modern lizards and other reptiles sometimes grow scutes. These are hardened, tough pads that are almost like bony calluses. In *Stegosaurus*, scutes covered much of the body. These scutes would have acted as body armor for *Stegosaurus*. The creature's throat was well covered with scutes, and the hip areas were extensively covered with this tough armor. Both hips and throat are

Attacked by a predator, *Stegosaurus* turns its back to the meat-eater and uses its tail spikes to defend itself.

prime targets for predators. This explains why *Stegosaurus* had thicker armor at these points.

Stegosaurus's relatives also featured scutes for body armor. Many of them had a system of defensive spikes that was far more elaborate than the tail spikes of *Stegosaurus*.

The skull of *Stegosaurus* resembled a sturdy rectangular box. The front of the snout ended in a horny beak. As the top and bottom came together when the dinosaur fed, they actually sharpened the beak's cutting edges against each other.

Chewing took place deep inside the animal's mouth. Rows of simple teeth lined the jaws and were replaced often as they wore down during the animal's lifetime. A groove in *Stegosaurus*'s jaw suggests the animal had strong, pouchy cheeks. *Stegosaurus* may have packed its cheeks full of food, then chewed it over and over to break down the plant fibers.

With a narrow skull and simple teeth, *Stegosaurus* probably browsed on soft plants. Some think it may have been able to rear up on its tall hind legs to reach foods. It would have used its thick tail for support as it did this. But most scientists think *Stegosaurus* fed mainly on plants three feet (1 m) tall or shorter.

This page: *Stegosaurus* shown with newly laid eggs. The mother will cover them with plant matter and leave them buried until they hatch. Opposite page: It's dangerous to leave the safety of the forest. And it's hard to take a drink when you're constantly on the alert for predators.

Food Aplenty

Stegosaurus's teeth and its low stance limited what the dinosaur could eat. Cedar, cypress, and sequoia trees were common when *Stegosaurus* lived. But they were far too tall to be a source of food. So what did this 30-foot-long (9 m), two to three ton (1.8–2.7 t), plant-eating dinosaur feed on?

The lush climate of that time supported a family of plants called cycads. These were tree-like plants with wood bark and simple branches. They resembled short palm trees. Most grew close to the ground and may have been an important food source for *Stegosaurus*.

Ferns flourished in the Jurassic. Some ferns even grew as large

This page: *Stegosaurus* may have used its tail and hind legs to support itself while it fed from higher branches. Opposite page: A *Stegosaurus* walks through the mist of a forest in search of food.

When attacked by *Ceratosaurus*, *Stegosaurus* turns to display its defensive weapons. A predator would have to be very hungry to risk being spiked.

as modern trees. *Stegosaurus* probably included soft Jurassic ferns in its diet. It may have also fed on tubers and the roots of certain plants, but we have no direct evidence for this. But regardless of what it ate, *Stegosaurus* must have spent much of its time feeding to keep its huge belly full.

Giant Neighbors

Stegosaurus was just one kind of plant-eating dinosaur that lived during the late Jurassic. The dominant plant-eaters of the age belonged to the sauropod family. These dinosaurs became the tallest, longest, and heaviest animals to ever walk the earth.

Stegosaurus and its cousins all had fairly long necks. But the sauropods took long necks to an extreme. *Diplodocus* was a six-ton (5.5 t) sauropod. It was 90 feet (27 m) long, 30 feet (9 m) of which was its neck. Despite its long neck, *Diplodocus* probably fed on soft, low-lying plants. If so, *Diplodocus* and *Stegosaurus* may have desired the same food. Rather than compete, the two animals may have occupied different areas of the prehistoric land. Flat, open river deltas may have been the territory of *Diplodocus* and other sauropods. Upland areas that might be hillier or more forested might have

Other animals with whom *Stegosaurus* shared its world. Here, the deadly predator *Allosaurus* attacks another plant-eater. It is a baby *Diplodocus*, one of the four-legged sauropods.

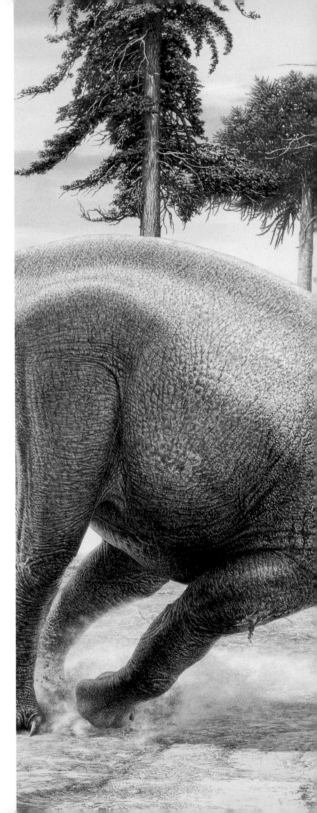

been favored by *Stegosaurus*. Curiously, sauropod and *Stegosaurus* fossils are seldom found together.

Like other plant-eaters, *Stegosaurus* had a variety of defenses to cope with predatory dinosaurs. Its scales were toughened into shield-like plates that defended its hips and its throat. The animal's skin was probably very thick, and this also served as a line of defense.

But it was the spikes on *Stegosaurus*'s tail that were probably its best weapons. The bones in the tail were very flexible. This would have made it easy to flip the tail from side to side. A *Stegosaurus* probably did not charge an attacker. Its best defense may have been to stand its ground. Digging in with its front legs and quickly twisting its rear legs, *Stegosaurus* could have flicked its spiked tail for defense. A direct blow would have crippled a charging attacker. This probably discouraged many predators.

Kentrosaurus (right) lived at the same time as *Stegosaurus* (above), but in a different part of the world. This African stegosaurid was about half the size of *Stegosaurus* but was equally well protected with plates and spikes. Here, the shadow of a predator falls across its flank, the most vulnerable area of a *Kentrosaurus*.

Few predators picked on *Kentrosaurus*. This stegosaurid, found in Africa, was like a prehistoric porcupine. A row of small triangular plates quickly gave way to increasingly large spikes that extended down the creature's back. Eight pairs of spikes covered its back, and an extra pair covered its front shoulders.

When asked to picture the classic dinosaur battle, most people think of *Tyrannosaurus rex* and *Triceratops*. Like *Triceratops*, *Stegosaurus* was an armored plant-eater. It lived long before the time of *Tyrannosaurus*, but it, too, shared the land with a monstrous predator. It was a fearsome meat-eater called *Allosaurus*.

The 35-foot-long (10.6 m), two-ton (1.8 t) *Allosaurus* had a large brain. It had powerful hind legs and strong arms. Each arm ended in a three-fingered hand with 10-inch (26 cm) claws. It is possible that *Stegosaurus* was an occasional meal on *Allosaurus*'s menu.

Ceratosaurus was another hunter that may have fed on *Stegosaurus*. This meat-eater was about the same size as *Allosaurus* and featured a horn above its nose. *Cerato-saurus* is thought to have been a pack hunter. An *Allosaurus* or a *Ceratosaurus* would have taken advantage of an injured or a young *Stegosaurus*. Easy prey like that is like a free meal to a predator.

Predators such as *Allosaurus* had to be careful when attacking armored plant-eaters. If they were wounded and could not hunt, they would die. And stegosaurids were well protected. But a related group of plant-eaters put them to shame. They were called ankylosaurs, and they looked like armored tanks.

Ankylosaurs were later cousins of the stegosaurids. They were the other major group of dinosaurs with bony armor. These were low, wide dinosaurs. They had armored backs, legs, and throats. Some had bony plates over their eyelids.

Two types of ankylosaurs existed. One type had an armored

This page: *Allosaurus*, a deadly predator that lived in the same time and place as *Stego-saurus*. Opposite page: A later group of arm-ored dinosaurs were the ankylosaurs. Here, one of them, *Talarurus*, defends itself with its heavy tail club.

knob at the end of its tail. *Ankylosaurus* and *Talarurus* are good examples. The armor covering their bodies was for defense. Their tail clubs were for offense. If a predator attacked, these dinosaurs could tail-whack it and send it packing.

The other group of ankylosaurs had no tail knobs. Instead, they relied on armor and spikes for protection. *Hoplitosaurus* was an ankylosaur from this group. Spikes ran along the side of the animal's tail. Solid armor in the form of scutes covered its back. Spikes lined its ribs.

Like the stegosaurids, ankylosaurids were probably not fast-moving animals. Both of these plant-eating groups relied on their armor. And both were quite successful.

Stegosaurus, and many of its plated and spiky cousins, became extinct about 140 million years ago. Many members of the stegosaurid family become extinct just as flowering plants began to dominate the land. Flowering plants may have taken over the places where ferns and other *Stegosaurus* favorites used to grow. Or perhaps the appearance of flowering plants signaled a change in the environment. This change would see the end of *Stegosaurus* and many other Jurassic dinosaurs.

But stegosaurids were a very successful dinosaur group. Their fossils show they lived in North America, Europe, Africa, and Asia. Stegosaurids lasted for about 50 million years.

A young *Stegosaurus* shares its domain with the giant sauropod *Brachiosaurus*. There's plenty of its favorite plant food around, but this will soon change, and *Stegosaurus* will soon disappear.

30

GLOSSARY

Allosaurus (AL-uh-SAWR-us): an allosaurid. The most fearsome predator of the Jurassic period.

ankylosaurs (an-KIE-luh-sawrz): group of plant-eating armored dinosaurs with low, barrel-shaped bodies.

Ankylosaurus (an-KIE-luh-SAWR-us): largest member of the ankylosaurids. An armored plant-eater.

Apatosaurus (uh-PAT-uh-SAWR-us): a sauropod plant-eater. One of the heaviest animals yet discovered.

Brachiosaurus (BRAK-ee-uh-SAWR-us): a large sauropod, with longer front legs than hind legs and a giraffe-like stance.

Ceratosaurus (ser-AT-uh-SAWR-us): a meat-eating dinosaur with a horn on its snout.

Diplodocus (di-PLOD-uh-kus): a sauropod. One of the longest dinosaurs, with a long neck and a long whip-like tail.

extinct (ik-STINKT): no longer existing.

fossil (FAH-sill): a remnant of a living organism that has turned to stone over time.

herbivore (URB-uh-vor): any plant-eating animal.

Hoplitosaurus (ho-PLEET-o-SAWR-us): an ankylosaur covered in armor and spikes.

Huayangosaurus (hwah-YAHNG-o-SAWR-us): a

stegosaurid with long shoulder spikes.

Kentrosaurus (KEN-tro-SAWR-us): a stegosaurid covered in eight pairs of spikes with another pair on its front shoulders.

predator (PRED-uh-tor): an animal that hunts and eats other animals for food.

pterosaurs (TERR-uh-sawrz): flying reptiles from the Mesozoic era.

sauropods (SAWR-uh-podz): a group of four-legged, plant-eating dinosaurs.

scutes (SKOOTZ): external armor made of thickened calluses.

stegosaurids (STEG-uh-SAWR-idz): family of dinosaurs with bony plates covering their bodies and spikes on their tails.

Stegosaurus (STEG-uh-SAWR-us): an armor-plated, plant-eating dinosaur.

Talarurus (tal-uh-ROOR-es): an ankylosaur with a bony knob at the end of its tail.

Triceratops (try-SER-uh-tops): a ceratopsid dinosaur with a three-horned face, powerful beaked jaws, and a short, bony frill.

tubers (TYOU-berz): short (sometimes underground) stems with small leaves and buds, able to produce new plants.

Tyrannosaurus rex (tie-RAN-uh-SAWR-us REX): a tyrannosaurid. One of the largest meat-eaters that ever lived.